THE POET'S PERFORMANCE

OF LIFE AND DEATH

The Poet's Performance of Life and Death

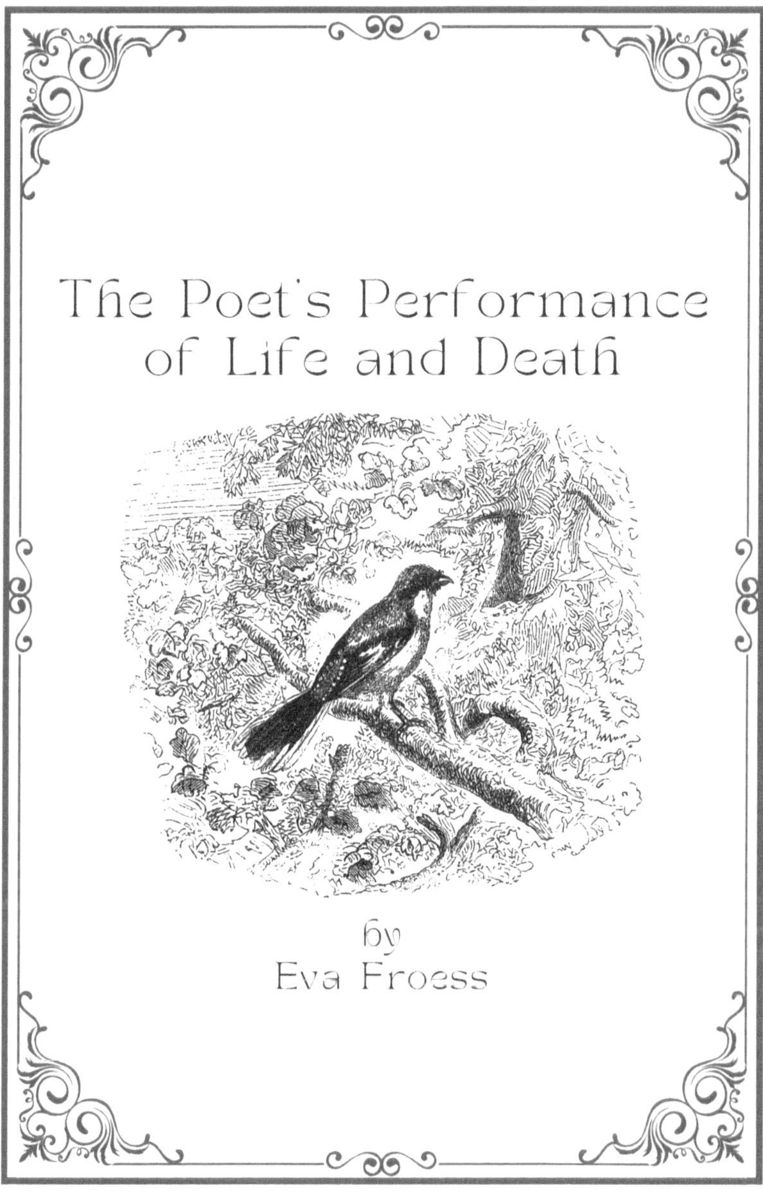

by
Eva Froess

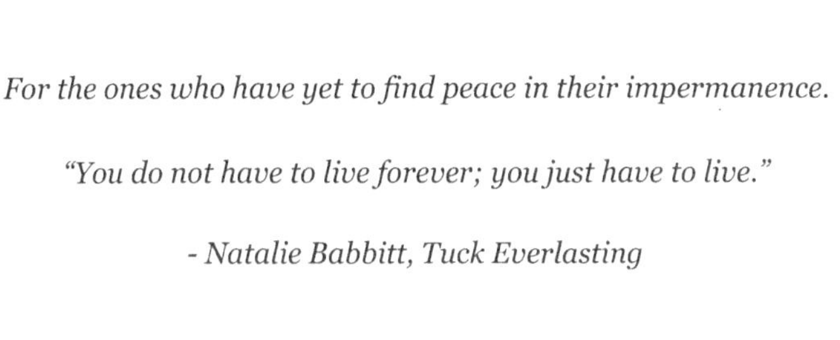

For the ones who have yet to find peace in their impermanence.

"You do not have to live forever; you just have to live."

- Natalie Babbitt, Tuck Everlasting

I

II

III

IV

I

BEING SEEN

Isn't it funny how we string
strange squiggles together on a page
and these little things
can hollow your chest,
or tug muscles in your cheeks?
I've always found it absurd
that this entanglement of twenty-six possibilities
creates a space for the frosted parts of myself.

Am I inside these threads?
Is this where my soul is when my body is vacant?
What a delicate thing it is
to make a home in your tracing eyes.

Thank you, reader.
Thank you for knowing me.

DANDELION SONG

I was born from a line of those who go
tufts to the wind beck and call, although
they float away.
Roots aren't things we make.

Die in the fall,
bounce back in the spring
mistaken for daisies
and nicer things

It's the bed we made
sunlight in the shade

Though I've never had a traveller's heart
make amends before faults
have reason to rot away
all the good things I've made in my time
droplets of sun come back
in a bitter light

I’ve never been the prettiest thing
Petals mistaken
for evergreen weeds
Taken to the wind
All for what they wish

Make no mistake
For I know what I am
The purpose I’m given from kind little hands
Whisper what you hope
Take my heart home

Though I've never had a traveller’s heart
Resting came after the last bits had rot
I’ll wear my lion crown
Light born from new ground
Trying something new
Back in the early spring bloom

I was born from a line of those who go
Small pieces go off, take wind, take hold
I think I find it sweet
Sunlight on your cheek
From me?

IMAGINARY SANCTUARY

One day, I will greet the 5 AM sunshine
at my unpolished kitchen table,
sat across from
a person I will share the rest of my life with.

They will smile at me, and it will be gentle.
Their parted lips won't drip
with poison, and I will not feel regret
when I kiss them goodbye.

I will have children who are not
cautious in connection,
and they will be unfamiliar
with fear.
Their lives will be joyful,
and there will never be a question
of if they are loved.

TO WHO WE WERE

As grateful as I am
to have met you at all,
there are many parts of my life I wish you could have seen
before we outgrew our imaginations.
I wish I could bring you to the tree I befriended when I was young,
or to the edge of my backyard, where I shared smiles
with the neighbour's dog-
he was always the best boy and a genius. He told me so.

I wish I had saved you a seat at the kid's table
during Thanksgiving when our adults could
fizzle their words through their teeth
then reconvene for pie and a glass of pinot noir.
We would be in the living room with full bellies,
taking turns drawing on the same piece of lined paper;
stick figures of my mom, brother, and sister outlining
a perfect recreation of your cat.

I wish we could have been school friends
so we could play dodgeball, get picked last,
then take each other to the nurse for an ice pack.
I wish I could have soothed your first bruise,
and you could have tidied my bloody nose.

I wish we could have been close
when our faces became rough as gravel.
I would have shared my home remedies
in exchange for a page in your puberty guidebook.
We would have been as much of a team back then as we
are now.

Time cannot move in reverse
and sending wishes back then doesn't work
the way it does for our future days.

I wish when we are old,
our house will be decorated with lined canvas art
recklessly crafted by our grandkids or our friends' kids that
live next door,
never condemning their creations to the fridge,

letting them blossom in loves full view
against our hallway walls.
I wish that when we are old,
we can be the local eccentrics that make an adventure
out of a journey to the pharmacy for my pain medication,
and whatever you have recreationally prescribed.

I want to be so intertwined with you,
our imaginations combine and create something only we
can see.
I wish I got to be young with you,
though I know we will not get old alone.

HOLY HOLLOW

I wish I could believe in a God
a higher power
something wiser
someone moral.
I wish my prayers
were not an echo ringing in my chest.

I wish I could touch the skin of a god
to feel the grit
of humanity pumping in their veins.

To have faith is to be
blindly guided into life unsure.

Is God a part of me?
A compass inside my aching bones,
something smarter,
someone silent?
Is wishing an act of prayer?

I've lived in an empty temple,
and I will die there too.

TO THE EARTH & BACK TO HER

I want to live a gentle life
tucking myself into bed, cozy and warm
just as my mother did
and her mother before that.

I want to feel every ray of sun absorbed into my skin
remind me of the warmth in the world
in the smaller bits.

I'll braid my hair-
recalling my femininity in each pleat
and I'll put serums and toners and lotions on my face
not in fear of my age beginning to show,
but to feel safe in my semi-permanent space.

I'll walk outside barefoot early in the spring
feeling each blade of grass crunch beneath my feet
though I will mind every bug & such
as they were here long before me.

and in the winter,
when it's difficult to be gentle
on the day of the first snowfall
I'll stir my tea four times clockwise
and *dink and clink* my spoon
on a frosted window sill pane.

MEMENTO MORI

In the stillness of late December
Oh, the mighty revenants that surround us
They come to us clockwork this time of year

Inwards, billowing whispers chant aimlessly.
For now and always, what remains
Are we whole, will we eternally be
Will there be life after breath and bone returns home

It's foolish to believe that these voices can be heard
There is no blaring intercom
to blanket their words over us
nor do they have breath to spew from
They are carcasses
with hollow twisting tongues
writhing omens from oral caves
We cannot hear their pother over mortality

They're inside of us
Carefully cradled in slick shame and knee-high snow
viciously snapping at our ankles
subvocally pleading for our lips to sound

in their name-

for something greater than nods and pity

In this living graveyard

we chatter and pretend we are weightless

unbound to our final destination

as they pull at us desperately

For now and always, what remains

Are we whole, will we eternally be

Will there be life after breath and bone returns home

Don't you find they get louder when the cold is pillowed?

WARMTH

I am grateful
I have embedded you
enough into my life
that finding the toothpaste
is second nature.
top left drawer, next to the bobby pins
You would repeat my directions in your voice,
though I don't hear you whisper it anymore.

I am grateful that the space I fear
so deeply when I am one
has become familiar to you.
There is no fear
when cooking yourself a meal.
You've learned I'll make too much
if you've been hungry for too long.
I don't need to pass you the salt and pepper;
you grab it with ease in our midnight meals.
You've come close enough to my life
to know it in its simplistic bits.

RECESS RULES

Within this lifetime,
we are all just kids
in a long-run playground game.

We are laughing at it all
crying over scraped knees
closing our eyes
counting to ten,
waiting for the next round to begin.

We play pretend in suits
over lunch break
and avoid the ever-growing,
everlasting,
not-so-nice peer at all costs.

No one ever leaves their wonder.
We are all just playing pretend.

NATAUSHA

A bubble-breathed woman invites herself
into your moment of silence
ash feathers down to her proudly bargained boots, from a talkative cigarette-
Lightly lipstick kissed,
more of a prop in her pub-broken advice.
She can feel your charred edges
you're burning just as much as her pack of conversation starters.
Her neck crooks with each stubborn response you offer back to her.
You can tell she sees right through you,
as if the polka-dots on her dress mirrored a clear view to your heartstrings
letting her feel it all *for* you.

She is no stranger to holding things that hurt.

Before parting ways permanently,
she shreds the last of your conversation
beneath her shoe and tightens her voice to say

When you've grown too far into the dirt
The only thing that'll make you nearly human again
Is to climb a tree and jump.

SPOKEN AT THE KITCHEN TABLE

With candles
and giggles
and half cold plates,
somehow, every word said
is disturbingly soft.
It's warm,
and each shoulder
has another to lean on.

It would be impossible
not to think
I am home
when the stories around you
are building roofs
and tearing down old walls.

GROWING HOME

I found myself crumbled overtop a garden.
Though it was no longer a garden,
but a sidewalk placed in spirals.
Never-ending,
almost routine.
I walked that path until my body gave out
and only the bleak stretched out farther
and farther ahead of me
until a shimmer of purple and evergreen
gently wrapped around my shoe.
Almost calming, nearly alive.

This flower introduced itself as clematis
though I knew its name,
I had an ear to listen.
It told me of it's journey beneath the pavement;
how cold and dark it'd been-
how my warmth had called it out
foolishly believing I was the sun.

As our introduction came to a natural end,
the clematis offered me one of their flowers.

Grow me somewhere new,
she asked.
Get us home together.
So we did.

For now, I was never travelling alone.
The pavement perished,
decorated with vines
and pockets of pillowed petals.

We made it home together.

A bed of fresh soil placed along the fence
gave room for each of us to grow.

As seasons change, frost is guaranteed.
The snow will cradle us both,
our colours never fading,
and we both will grow a home.

GIRLHOOD

No one ever grows out of girlhood
Womanhood is just a "grown-up" term
an excuse to wear heels
and dig into our mothers' makeup
the colours are more vibrant
when it doesn't belong to you.

Girlhood will always leave
a wad of bubblegum
ratted in our hair
sticking to our hearts
a residue behind our ears because
"Violet Beauregard did it"
and to that, we followed.

It is the thick air
haunting your best friend's bedroom
a reminder of the concentrated laughter
and secrets and truth
spoken the night before.

You can nearly hear
the confessions
bouncing off of each others'
childhood stuffed bears-
tucked into your school bags, safe and sound.

It's hidden in kitchen cupboards
impulse-bought mugs and
chipped ceramic bowls
from the night you made soup,
and things got *hectic*.

It's tucked away,
pillowed in your blankets
the smell of cheap body mist,
summer sun, and somehow an aroma
from the spontaneous beach trip
and the sweaty singing car ride there.

In this moment, you realize
how absorbent girlhood is,
though seemingly impermeable.

I know most wish to go back
longing for their beginning
with a twinge of regret
　　　　I'd hold on longer
　　　　maybe forgive her family
　　　　eating ones' sharpened words
　　　　wanting to try again.
But isn't that girlhood in itself?
Believing in re-dos,
begging to be understood?

GROWING UP TOGETHER

The morning after I spent being young
with the people I grew up with,
salvaging the feelings from what
we remember,
groggy and hobble-footed
I floated to the bathroom
to wash the wine-tinted morning breath away,
remembering a joke someone had made about
how all of us are filled with helium,
with no strings to tie us down.
It was really more of an observation.

Running the toothbrush in spirals on my smile,
I can't avoid a cheeky expression or two in the mirror.
I tug my shoulders back,
and in a passing glance
I catch a second of a reflection that is not of mine
but of my mothers,
twenty years before today.

The thing that drew me to certainty
that it was my mother staring back at me
was a bug-eyed infant bouncing
up and down,
and up and down,
and up and down on her hip.
It's hard to miss such jarring eyes,
when my mother's are of emerald and gold.

In her arms, she's bobbing me up and down
and brushing her teeth,
wiping the tired from her eyes,
and then from mine.

I wonder if she also felt
too young to be grown
or if the creak of adulthood
was followed by baby monitors and
a sore hip.

I wish we didn't have to grow up together.

FINDERS KEEPERS

Your eyes match the sunny shimmer
that smiles its way through
a willow tree
onto the dirt,
with our backs laid gently against it.

I could see the earth in your eyes,
as it echoed through your words
on how we could save it.

Somehow, the forest befriended the ocean.
I think that's the best adventure.

A HOW-TO GUIDE:
RESURRECTING YOURSELF

I.) Eat something.

I don't care what it is. It doesn't matter. The first step is the most important, yet most of us forget (or choose not to). Burn the ideology that to be fully alive, you must not eat a thing. Scrap anything negative that has been spoken through sharp teeth with a romantic twist. If you must be poetic about it, share an orange with someone you love. Eat something that reminds you that you are human.

II.) Smile at yourself.

Not your planned, picture-ready smile. Ugly smile in the mirror- smile until you no longer believe it to be ugly. If you must, conjure up a joke your dad told you when you were young and the belly laughter following the initial wince. Picture your friend smiling, and how sweet their laughter sounds in combination with yours.

When a mammal bares their teeth, we see it most through a snarl. When people smile, it's usually an attempt at non-verbally saying:

I am safe, and you can trust me.

You deserve to see yourself in a secure light. You deserve the kindness exuded from your own smile.

III.) Create something.

Art and creation are such subjective areas, and sometimes, to understand why you're feeling the way that you are, you have to make it first. Deciphering your own thoughts is a mind trick. Sometimes, you don't know what you're feeling until you can look at it, or hold it, or read it.

MAGPIE'S ECHO

I look for you on trails I hike
hidden in trees
scribbled in their bark-
small secrets of before I was new

in the radio silence
I can nearly hear your name
cawed from magpies
frolicking near my heartbeat

I can almost hear you
calling from around the bush
swallowed by the wonder
of freshly faced old memories

it's warm
I can almost feel you with me
sun rays can mimic the call of a hug
you're right here
somewhere between what I am now
and who I might have been

POMEGRANATE

There is delicacy in the time it takes for us to die.
Every second can be savoured,
catching each pomegranate seed
between the molars we hide,
savouring what we know will be gone
our labours are put to rest.

Our fingers stick kindly to each thing we greet afterwards
a call from the gentleness of before sweetly saying
I am still here.
I still remember.

The husk has never been something to hide.
The tough parts always make the first bite feel generous
and worthwhile.
There is a delicacy in what we know as a chance,
serenity in what pains us to feel,
a glimmer in the destruction.
Love is found in the small bits.

I know your laugh
and in every lifetime
it'll follow me
through the magpies.
I’d build a nest
for them
though every late fall
they will fly away
for something new.

WHEN ALL IS STILL, WE CRACKLE

Each night
A visitor comes knocking-
Unlike a vampire
The visitor does not wait for a welcome
He always finds his way in.

You have tried boarding the windows
Changing the locks
Yet he always finds his way back in
Sitting quietly at the fireplace.
Never in the way, but always watching.

You began to think he was only a nightmare
or else some sad excuse for a ghoul
But you have been close enough to touch his skin
and feel the chill of his breath
On the front of your neck.

Never in the way,
but always watching.

The sun has risen.

Nothing bleeds forever.

It’s warm,

And scabs are a reminder of spring.

SUNNY-SIDE UP

It's the little things I miss with you.
The grand adventures were amazing,
but my favourite things were scattered
through smaller moments.
Like the one time we both returned to the childhood
bone-chill from the dark. Neither of us fearless,
and in that moment, you scavenged all the courage you had
to walk to the place you'd slept
avoiding saying 'your bedroom' as your bedroom
was my bedroom. We both know that.
to grab your salt lamp.
It's the things we couldn't say, but the things we could do,
with me and you.

The morning after, we all made breakfast, and you
giggled every time you passed me a burnt hash brown.
Regardless, we still made breakfast.
You laughed that the eggs were cold and 'sunny.'
it's the things we couldn't say,
but the things we could do,
with me and you.

II

MUG RINGS

We are scars on each others' hearts.
Who we are now remembers who we were together
before our first smile lines.
One does not remember their own, only the visual from the other.

When we were young, however,
I have freckles on my arms that bloomed our first summer.
They've been with me for years,
some as small as the world felt to us.

Every winter, we have laid in the freshly fallen snow
and bled out together
    Cracking each other's chests open
    going for the heart
because we made an unspoken promise that no one freezes alone.
    Even when we were cruel,
    the knife was always double-sided.

When we agreed to be gentle,
that time is documented
in mug rings on each other's nightstands.
  Hot chocolate is sweet-
  almost as sweet as we had been.

Everything we have ever shared,
everyone we have ever been,
is ingrained into the other.
So, no matter the distance,
I hope you can see me and remember
that we were girls together.

AUGUST: XIV

standing on the cliff of youth
staring below
at the cooling promise of my future
all I wanted to do
was shout as loud as my lungs would allow

we are young now,

and with you my heart will never age!

FOUR YEARS AHEAD, FOUR STEPS BEHIND

I'm teaching you how to ride a bike.
The courage came entirely from you,
as I'd feared you would scrape your knee and never come
to know
your first slice of freedom.

When you started to grow,
I did my best to remind you
that it isn't your job to be pretty.

I'd take the risk of the lecture
that followed some
silly pink lipstick
stained in the carpet,
and to the apples of your cheeks.

I tried to show you
that your only job is to *feel* your life,
to let it be entirely yours.

I still remember the last time
you needed my hand to wander safely,
and the first time you said
        I'm a big girl! I can go alone.

But if the time ever comes
that you want my hand
to hold yours into the world,
a big sister never goes far

        I'm only ever four steps ahead,
and you are only four steps behind.

MOSCATO BREATH

I've been so caught up
in the world that bustles in my brain
to hear the universe
that blooms outside.
I'm dancing around the kitchen
I'm moving my limbs against the air
that feathers your smile.

I forget that the 'big things'
don't compare half as well
as getting a little wine drunk and
sharing a laugh with you.

THE THINGS WE SAID

The things you said at 1 A.M.-
with your head on my chest
and a singular heartbeat
shared between two.

The things I said too quietly-
sweetness coated in thick concern
the bits that slipped
past us both.

The words exchanged
when we were both broke down-
clinging to the bathroom sink
praying that whatever we said
would sound elegant
and not too desperate.

All of these things lead back
to our first kiss-
the thing I've been
repeating over and over again,
I've been waiting for you my whole life.

CONFESSIONARY

To fall in love is to say
    I will show you who I am now,
    and I will allow myself to change with you.
It is to break every single security measure
that you've spent decades crafting
and to be seen to your rotten core.

It is the act of allowing every version of yourself
to meet every version of them.
The mirrorball children,
the misunderstood, no-good teens,
and the larger-than-life old ages
when your bones just aren't like they used to be.

To love another person is to bandage wounds
they've had long before you
that never seem to scab up, and always bleed through.
Loving is a painful game,
and I hope you'll never stop playing.

ODE TO A GHOST

I realized I was in love with you on our third date.
It was titled: Christmas movies in our pyjamas
our fingers intertwined, matching the pattern
of our pants.
I knew it then,
that I would be happy doing this
for as long as time allowed us,
for as long as time could promise,
at least until the end of the credits.

I didn't say it then,
though I'm glad I didn't
because today,
as we drove home
from a concert neither of us could comprehend,
I felt the overwhelming urge
to remind you that
I love you.

that I love you so much my heartbeat
matches yours without my effort
that I've picked up your quirks
and I keep them in my pocket
wishing you can see all these things
you hate
in a warmer light.

I stared out the window
tracing the trees with my fingertips
the evergreens counting the seconds in my head
thinking I may look foolish
and that my words would stumble
out of my mouth messily
like a love-drunk poet
fearing that what I might say would appear hesitant
I did try my best.

for a moment, I worried that the silence would continue
and you would have nothing to say
but then I realized I was happy just knowing that you knew
that *you* are loved
that's all I needed
and all my caution of the phrase

faded out of view with the traffic signs.
all I could see ahead of me was the hope that you knew
illuminating in the sun rays beaming through the
windshield

I hope you know.

I'm so glad you exist.
I'm glad I exist, too,
and I'm grateful that the world has been kind enough
to let us experience our lives
in the same timeline.
I hope this gets through to you.

PRIOR ST.

On the corner of Prior and Pleasant,
a quaint blue house stands,
framed by peeling picket fences,
encasing grass that's grown wild and high.
A rusted red Ford rests beside it,
deep in slumber,
it's metal slowly consumed by spring's embrace,
petals drifting like memories around it.

Flowers bloom from cracks in weathered panels,
while ivy climbs the corners,
reaching for a touch of sun.
Is this place always alive?
Has death ever brushed against the stillness
of this quiet corner of the world?

Though none of us tread bare-footed on the floorboards,
inside, a hush envelops the air—
yet Prior pulses with life,
each whisper of wind, each rustle of leaves,
a reminder that even in silence,
this corner breathes,
holding stories in its gentle grasp.

A POET'S HAND

I figured I would try and paint something
extraordinary
or scramble my feelings into chocolates
far too bland to be tasteful
but nothing else seemed to fit-
other than a poem.
You are a poem I have dreamed of writing
since the first time I picked up a pen
How could one write something of love true to its form
without knowing what it was.
        You are my poem.
Perhaps my favourite so far.
I want to write about the glimmer in your eye
the one that shimmers the brightest
when recalling your little brother
or maybe your smile that you swore you never share
but I broke the second I met you
I want to write all the things that have been
ingrained into my memory
        but you, in your own being
        are my favourite poem.

SUN-STAINED LIPS

This morning, I woke up in your arms
slightly sweaty
with the sun tingling my face
and you kissed me
and I did not flinch
or lean away
and in that moment,
I could only help but to think
that I would stay here forever if given the chance.
A perfect entanglement.

OVER & ONWARD

I love you to death
isn't enough
I love you past death
and into the abyss
or at least the next life.

I'll love you with every first and last breath
that escapes my lungs

I love you with every fibre of my being,
every strand of hair,
and every cell of blood.

I'll love you until time stops,
even then,

time is theoretical.

SOFTLY AT SEA

There isn't much point
in longing for something I've said goodbye to,
something we have both sent off sailing
but you,
I hope you don't let the love I built for you
end up shipwrecked.
Let it be the wind in the cotton sail.
Let your waters be calm and glassy.
Let yourself be loved.

If time takes hold
and fate has us rest on the same shore,
look to the sand for an old moscato bottle
there, you will find what we've lost.

All it will read,
underneath the spilled ink and secrets is
I hope you get to be happy sometimes
and my home address
in case you ever want to stop by.

TAKE HEED

I swear I had never heard a single sound before I met you.
My ears had learned to dampen all resonance
as nothing could be worth the ringing in my head
I had enough of that on my own accord.
Voices were hollow vibrations,
music was bleak,
that's that.

Though somehow, now I'm sitting with my cheek on your shoulder,
feeling each chord pull through each tiny muscle
up to where my face lays.
Sound was born from you-
as far as I'm concerned.
Music lives and shines from you
and I want to feel every note, lyric, and sound like you do.
I heard my name for the first time when you said hello,
and it was the sweetest thing.
You are the sweetest sound.

ORANGE

I hope my hands never grow stiff
my joints hardening in time
the clock may have all other bumps and bends
but my hands are mine.
With my hands, I can paint pictures
details of a vibrant life
I can hold your face when you are crying
my hands soothe you
as your hands do mine.

With my fingers, I hold the world
every word in each nerve
with my fingers, I write stories
something to recite before bed
details safe and sound.

Though the thing I most dread
in the worry of losing my hands
is when we are old and tired
peeling your oranges will be a chore.

When we've aged and time has taken
each bit of grace I've ever owned
it may take my voice- that I'll allow
as the clementine says much more.

I know your indifference with citrus
never too much of a fan
though I hope when we're old
we can each have a half
that I've split with my hands.

I'm sure that I'll always be able
to peel each part away for you
though never do I wish it to be messy
I was taught young
how to make the peel a flower
detailing with the star-shaped stem.

My love for you is a taste
as strange as that sounds
it's fresh and bright
like the first summer
we fell into each other.

When the world meets its end
the last thing I hope I am to do is
split an orange with you.

I hope to always feel the stickiness
on my fingertips
and the acidic tingle on my lips
in those, I know home
in those, I've felt what love is.

Share an orange with me,
let's learn what good love tastes of.

THE ART OF KNOWING

you keep a list
of the things that slip out of my mouth
when I am content
Oh, I like that
this one's my favourite and so on.

I've learned to speak to fill space
or to not speak at all
so when you casually said
that you keep the things I say documented
something became clear to me.

This is the first time
in a long time
that my words meant something to someone
that I meant something to someone
and how special it is
that it has been you.

A WRITER'S STUDY OF LOVE

January Third, 2024

I am sitting in a chain cafe with arguably the best person
I have ever met.
We pass back and forth a page covered in doodles
and questionable self-portraits.
My summer song played
in early January,
and I have my favourite drink.

I am so glad I am alive
and that change happens regardless
of what we do to stop it.
You are the sweetest thing.
I love the way you think.

——

January Tenth, 2024

I am sitting in a busy cafe
measly attempting to start writing again
attentive to what is living around me
forceful to feel everything.

there is a woman sat behind me
mirroring a scribbled version.
I wonder if I have caught too many glances
and she now knows she is the subject of what I write.

writers never see the muse of themselves-
I wonder if she's ever had
something written about her before.
the barista and her have matching star earrings
dangling through where their hair falls.
how simple and delicate people are
in the tiny details.
You would like her sweater.
it sticks out like a giggle in a library,
and that one coral-coloured shirt you own
among fabric callbacks to when you were thirteen,
misunderstood, and angry.
or my crimson-flushed cheeks
when you kissed me for the first time-
the glimmer in your eyes illuminating
my smile like it were streetlights.

I've fallen so hard for you
I see you even when I am trying not to.
You're in the cable knit of the writer behind me.

I ordered a london fog,
never veering from my usual order before
because your kiss tastes like earl grey
and vanilla.
They put a heart on top of it, too.
They knew I came to write about you.

———

January Eleventh, 2024

Twenty-four hours later,
I sit in the same cafe now across from you,
my beautiful muse.

I am stubborn with my writing-
I do not want to be just a lover
or one who sits solely in despair
I want to be more than one thing
I want to write about every drop of life.
however, despite my best efforts
I can only write of you.

NOVEMBER XVII

I am going to marry him.
            Telling this to you
            because these are things he can't hear.
            It'll get to his head.

I cannot wait to fall in love with him once a week,
and once more every time he plays the strings.
The ones of my heart, or the guitar?
Either or is fine. It feels all the same.

I can't wait to bicker, and apologize
after the shine in his eyes reminds me
it's the kind thing to do.
I want to be so good to him
that he will forget what bitter feels like
tasting the sweetest black coffee
as the smallest bit dribbles down his chin
in the race out of *our* front door.

I hope I get to keep explaining
poetry to him.
I know I'll never get bored.

GODISGOOD.COM

A billboard I passed on a long stretch
of nowhere, to a large town of nothing.
Before this, advertisements
for phone sex,
A lawyers way out of a loveless marriage,
and Arby's.
Not to mention the main attraction of
British Columbia

The heart, The home
The 'roll it up and deeply breathe'

Those things are everywhere nowadays.

But a website for God?
We've been getting inventive
with our word
and our preach
If god had a search bar,
what do you think we would see

In a glance over his shoulder
and past his seamless robe,
my best guess is Pinterest outfit inspo
and a board solely for
three-step fig sangria recipes
you can make on your own at home

Now, here's the question
that has stumped us dull
What would be in the tabs that God wouldn't log
I know most would assume nothing at most
Though I suppose if he acted in the creation us all
What would have stopped him from
Helping those billboards stand tall?
They were hidden in the middle
of nowhere, after all.

III

A WRITERS CURSE

I believe part of me is afraid of death
Or rather, the impermanence of my being
I am scared of my soul dying with my bones and blood
So I write.
I will write to keep my thoughts immortal
And at least some piece of myself in the minds of others.
My vulnerabilities
And feelings
And heart
Are intertwined into each word I write
And some part of that will carry on past me

I will write to belong,
I will write to be remembered.
I will write until my lungs stop, and even then, I'll
continue on.

OYSTER

I am alone.
My exterior deterring to most
that's not what they want, not me.

they'll expose my insides
cracking open my ribs
reaching in with a heavy hand
to dress it up on a platter
or a display to be hung around their neck
only then will I be just to their liking.

What is it that they really desire?
The stolen kindness birthed from a grain of sand.
I've fixed it.
I loved it.
They only want what I have made good.

THE FACE IS BLANK

I do not wish to remember your name

or your home address

the smell of your clothes

or how your left canine veered slightly to the right

I do not want to remember

how you made me laugh

or the sound of your dad's voice.

I do not wish to remember
who I was after you
either.

SECOND DEGREE

my eyes see people
crowds
beating hearts
but every other part of my body sees a fire
a burning building
that I am only expected to run into gracefully
these people that I see
can tell that I am drenched
head to toe
in gasoline
dripping from the tips of my fingers
like sweet, fresh honey
the fossilized stench deters them
but the flames do not part
It's shouts are not welcoming
crackling and hissing
every step I take closer
I shake.

IN CARE

I am infectious
infectious laughter
infectious smile
in fact
I am without my own disease
spreading into others
I am one to please

so, for all I radiate
is that what I lose?
the bright light that seeps out of me
why can't I have some of my own?

am I not strong enough to self-inflict
my infection
onto myself?

CHRISTMAS IN RECOVERY

Walking through town all alone,
 clenching your palms to melt off the cold
The city knows something you don't
 chanting through thistle and car horns and bells
The winter is calling you home.

On the phone, you know that they're one call away
It's not weak to reach out, dear.
Stay warm, stay safe.
The two-step they'll do has never been a game that you'll play.

Do you think they'll still want to connect after all the festivities have passed?
In January, they will lose your best joke
Having now seen you without your best coat
Darling, I know how you get when it starts to get cold.

You spent your first snowfall in a waiting room chair
Making small conversation with the man losing hair
Both cracking jokes about the dead-eyed reception
The two of you are the only ones laughing.

What is Christmas if not a place to put grief?
You murmur as ten digits highlight your vacant screen
We can talk about the weather
and your decorated tree
But they mustn't make the mistake
of asking how you've been
As that's a bridge you'll burn
just to rid your gums of the taste

I know it will feel familiar,
The free will of losing it all.

So you will try again in the spring
When your life doesn't feel like a trapdoor to escape
You'll barter and negotiate a call in autumn
By then, you'll have gift-wrapped
all that is left of yourself.

ANGEL SONG

I was gifted a music box from my mom when I was a kid
looking like an angel with a heavenly tune
I remember falling asleep to it
the song long enough to carry me into rest
into the morning, where the sun shined just for me
it was simple.
Every night, I looked forward to the promise of a melody
playing it through my head in the day,
it was longer then.

Hearing it now,
after the years of it's travel
being tossed and thrown
the knob turns backwards and shakes with each touch
it's too short,
and I've forgotten the notes
it doesn't play as smooth
more spurred and different from what I knew.

It will never play long enough
to bring back what it once was
it will never sound the same

and the angel's wings
will only be held together
with hot glue
and the light of youth.

VACANT BONES

become become become become

be whole, stay whole

be full

How sweetly it drips off the tip of your tattered tongue

intertwined with the skin on my chest

become

be new

stay whole

A tricky dance between you and I

You are athirst and insatiate

nothing filling the hollow and

angry and empty carcass that you are

feeding and tearing and digesting

what there is of me

more more more

sweetly suggesting I should *just say no*

when your sharp hands billow over my ribs

waiting for your next bite

I am whole.

Perhaps this is what it's supposed to feel like
The ache
The stretch of frail flesh.
What is made of me
is to be used or else savoured
Someone has to suffer

What makes me true is the indents
And carvings of you.

PATRIARCH WALTZ

You've never considered your father to be a good man,
though you believe he already knows
You imagine a conversation with him over a cup of black
coffee
bubbling thick steam across the table
you wish it to be spoken softy in the cold hush between
you both
when the resentment can be tasted in the air
and bitter brume, much the same as an anti-bite nail coat.
In this, you would say
you are not who you wanted to be
and it would be the most confident thing
you have ever said to him
Still, knowing your father
he would titter stiffly beneath his breath,
wringing his shoulders from his ears to remove
the statement caught between them
the air would return to its stagnant state.

Your father lives in this world of grey static,
birthing you into it as well

so you will talk about
the weather and grocery lists
and how things are tight for the both of you right now
because acknowledging how weak he has become would
address how he cannot handle the weight
of the world,
or the pressure of a son.

DEATH OF AUGUST

the world begins its turn from the deep oranges and crisp reds,
to what feels like worldwide isolation-
cold and muffled movement
and you have found yourself
folded against the tile floor, mirroring your shower wall
assuring yourself *I am good, I am soft, I am gentle*
but the same echo greets you every change in the seasons
expecting your own words in reverberation
a shiver is shot down your spine
hearing instead,
Are you sure? Are you certain? Is that definitive?

PAST / PRESENT

I broke your mug today
while washing your dishes-
attempting to be helpful.
My hands were covered in suds.
The water was warm,
and the mug was the last thing left to dry.

one dire second sent me back
to a place I can only hope of forgetting
when there were more dishes
that were not mine
but the wash had to be done.

I am young-
the handle shattered into three.
The water *is* warm
and the hand burned into my cheek
was almost the same.
My skin *was* warm.

The room I am in was different just a moment ago.

I'm in the corner
not sure of how I got here
my skin *was* warm,
but it isn't burning anymore
I was somewhere else just seconds ago.

It *is* loud
and you *were* quiet and I *am* warm
and I *was* not scared.
I was looking into your eyes
and I can hear the footsteps
shaking the ground in the room next to me.
I *am* holding my breath,
and you had *told me to breathe*.

I am time-jumping between good and bad
I had been somewhere else moments ago.
You *weren't* there, *and I wasn't here*.

The mug was gone
before I came to.
My skin was warm with forgiveness
and I am somewhere new.

SOFTLY SHAPEN

I want you to see me
as something untouchable–
when did you learn that my skin wouldn't burn yours
when did you ask to part the flames inside of me?

you said my skin was brumal and bitter
as marble would be to hold
that should have been enough to keep you away
when the living play dead
you're meant to depart from the dissipation
let the fallen ones lie

you are not supposed to touch the dead
certainly not with malicious palms
and nails sharp enough to slice through pleas

I want you to see me as untouchable
I am not yours.
the words I spoke were never meant for your violence
I am not yours.

I am a delicately crafted monument,
chiselled with a pick and a blade
to contain a hell that burns bright
that now resides deep within me.
My body is not yours to keep.

I am not for your hands.
I am untouchable.

CONTORTION

I am no stranger to making myself small-
trying to fill as little space as humanly possible.
I am a master at being tucked away
my identity, like pillow talk
and dainty white secrets-
something you know, but not well enough to cling to.
I have only known how to control the art of disappearing
crafted by my own hands;

Until I met you.
until my character became origami
my love suddenly the folds
you've made into the belly of a whale.
I wanted to love you loudly
and only then I *wanted* to shout

> *I do not want to be small! I want to make the*
> *world turn for you!*

though for the first time in a long time,
I was too much.
for the first time, not by my design

I was overbearing,

or a coward-

who I was, dependent on how *you* felt that day.

I didn't notice until I broke out

until I said enough

to someone shrinking me from the outside

until the art became unfamiliar,

until it hurt.

I don't ever want to be small again

not even by my own hand.

I will never let you feel in control of a life that is not yours-

a life that is all mine.

THE FALL OF FAIRYTALES

womanhood is one of the most beautiful ideas
young girls draw up in their minds.
though, that's just the trouble
It's a beautiful idea.

as those young girls grow,
so do the monsters in their closet
they come into the daylight and dress with a charming
smile,
guarding their pointed molars.
he will tell those half-grown girls that she's pretty,
the word morphing into more
vulgar things after a glass or two of cheap wine.

these monsters grow with her
never wavering in the same fear
only becoming more accustomed to it-
her attune. They'll learn to speak,
offer her a drink and a ride back to his place.
He will mock her femininity
in a way that sounds sweet,
and womanhood will feel a tad less homely.

You must know that these monsters
never change their behaviour.
what felt like beady eyes from under her bed-
growing and scheming
only followed her to her first date.

his gaze still feels like daggers,
and soon enough, she will come to realize
she never left her childhood room

the monsters welcomed themselves to the outside
and the beautiful ideas she made
will appear in her dreams,
and her sweetest ones alone.

LAIKA

the place smells of cracking paint
a highly saturated framed far,
far away
hangs loosely to the plaster
reading a bolded bon voyage
 as she sits and waits
the secretary has AM playing the news
 that they sent a dog to the moon
the caster's hopeful tone
brushes over the part
 where she can't come home

the chatter from the desk
starts spilling over
into the plastic-covered waiting room
about how times are changing
humanity might make it
            how this might just be it.

YOU WILL NEVER BE A GOD

rewrite
redo
rebecome
old testament starting new.
you are not a god-
hidden behind flesh, and mortality
beginning and ending with the rest of us.
you may believe you carry
the blessing of invincibility
surviving a bloodied throat,
and sunken ribs,
bible verses displayed on a scale
prayers tucked behind rotting teeth.
a god is large-
booming even
yet to be a god,
to you
feels small,
cold,
and ridged
and god does not shiver.

UNDONE

In some other universe
there's a version of you and I that stayed us
and for a while, I would cling to it
digging my nails into the idea
leaving torn words along a lightly damp page
as if I were a driven dog holding tight to my days

I don't find comfort in it anymore
I know this to be true
because I'm sitting in my room, and some mindless scroll
led me back to the idea
of "another universe"
and I felt a sickening curl in my stomach.
Ah ha, just now, I felt it
a release in the lead that strung me to you
With that,

I now get to let go.

MY MOTHER'S SKIN

I stand in front of a mirror-
sometimes, just a camera,
and a snarl forms on my face
rabid and choking
like a bullet in a stuffed bear.

in front of my mother, I'll say something sarcastic
truly just hatred towards my own skin
and my mother will snap back
Never with malice
but through it, she'll say
"You look just like me."

it's as if we are standing face-to-face with loaded guns
trying to threaten the realization
of beauty into each other
to notice we share the same skin
that she created mine.
I only see beauty when I look at my mom
and it's true,
I do look just like her
but if I despise my own,

just the same as she does hers
What does that make of us?

Do I share my mother's skin?
Is it something I should loathe
even though she looks at mine with care?
Why does my mom hate her own skin?
Why do I hate mine?

TO WHO IT MAY CONCERN

every poem I write is a eulogy
something someone can toss in
that captures who I am
framed with my *about-the-author* photo
filtered beyond recognition
like the ashes that will become of me.

every poem I write,
I am planning my funeral
each journal a graveyard of
what if's
and who could I have been's
but it's something that will make everything
just a tad easier for everyone around me
a bit more palatable, per se.

Perhaps a rule book on how to remember me

think of yours truly
in verses and lines.

REFLECTIVE WAYS

I do not wish to be the sun anymore.
I don't want to reflect off of you any longer.

I want you separate,
relying only on the moonshine.

I want to be the moon
I'll shiver,
and break from the continuous burning.
I'm burning for you-
ash beds as feet.

I do not want the light love that beams off my tongue
to never be words of your own.
I do not want my own love back
in a reflection of you.

IV

SCRAPBOOK

When I get caught in the bitter spiral of
who am I? Who was I? Who will I be?
I look to the finger-painted heart
I made in the second grade for valentines day
in the tiny prints,

I can see my family.
in the smears, I can feel every one
of their smiles
beam at it
only a decade and some later.

It is still there; I can still feel it.

I hold the first poem I wrote
touching the angst and smearing the ink
reading it now,
I am glad it never left the secrecy of my journal
though the ghost of someone
I no longer know
peeks through the previous page
with their advice on poetry for dummies.

They are still there; I can still feel it.
I ruffle through my old Polaroids
dropping one face up
exposing a photo I took of my best friend
baby-faced and their hands covered in Sharpie
I remember the rebellion
in their possible ink poisoning

I hold the glossed-over photo, tap my heels three times
and I'm back in that classroom,
getting smiley faces and flowers patterned on my arm
when only violence
had been that close to my skin,
kindness bloomed.
I am still there; I can still see it.

I realized,
while scavenging for my identity
in old pictures and papers
simply seeing it all was where I lie
who I am,
who I have been,
and whoever I'll be
is scattered through all

of the people and places and poems
I have ever loved
who I am is written on the back of receipt paper
in my friend and old-coworkers handwriting
recommending podcasts and bits of thoughts
she wanted to share with me while I was busy.
who I am is displayed on traffic cone yellow sticky notes
always reading something of well wishes
get home safe, eat something,
make good choices.
which I would then fold into butterflies,
simple and crafted.

in the countless Polaroids I have
they all have two things in common-
I took the photos, and I took them for a reason
never the subject, but I have always been there.
I will always be there,
behind the flash
illuminating what I love.

I am in the decade-old arts & crafts
cookie cutter projects
to keep an entire class tame.
harder to find in this one,
I look closer.
My fingerprints are in every drop of paint.

fearful I'll lose this epiphany as easily as before
I decide to take the glue, tape,
and tacks I've been using
to hold the faceless version of myself together,
and I began
a scrapbook.

202

when I was in middle school, I would walk
every morning through the neighbourhood
adjacent to mine. I would leave early
avoiding what I could of the morning rush of cars,
and people, and chaos
walking in the calm and quiet.

when the world was resting,
it was just myself
and the woman in mobile home #202 awake.
I knew nothing of her,
only the wilted flowers that hung underneath the window
she would sit at every morning
with the same teacup,
and the crown of her grey hair in velcro rollers.

I had always figured we were up then
for the same reason
finding solitude in the rising sun
until she started adding a beaming smile
to our passing wave
nearly excited for our daily encounter.

when it got cold,
and I was *too cool* for a jacket
one sat at the end of her driveway,
with a handwritten note in blue ink
smeared from the snow

'for the young woman who walks by,
this is an old coat of mine. It's too cold to only
wear a T-shirt.'

I didn't take the coat
moving it to her porch before
thanking her with a smile.
her kindness was unwavering
not knowing how far I'd come,
or how much longer I had left to go
just making sure I stay warm.
only then did I realize our days started early
for different reasons.
I was set out for empty company,
and she was observant of connection.

I had moved that year,
never saying a full hello or goodbye
to the woman in #202

frankly, it slipped my thoughts
until I drove by her house
a few years later
seeing a sold sign sat where the coat had once been
and a young family,
collapsing boxes
on a newly renovated porch
decorated meticulously with tulips and
shouts of spring.

wherever she is,
I hope she's warm.
I hope I learn her name one day.

I wish I had said hello
to the woman in #202.

GROWN-UP

I'll never be six years old again,
getting breakfast with my grandparents
in my princess dresses-
smiling back at my smiley-face pancakes.

I'll never be that ten-year-old
who found the utmost joy
sleeping on the floor
and running around in the mud
with the neighbourhood kids
who we weren't quite friends with
but we stuck together.

thirteen passed me by in a fit of rage,
and the phrase "troubled youth."
She felt so grown up while so small.

fifteen greeted me with eager hands
and friends I thought would last
through lifetimes.

in each, we would spend our time seated in a field
telling childhood stories
until the streetlights came on,
or one of us decided it was time to grow up.

at seventeen, I graduated high school
blissfully frightened, eager for life,
invincible to the world,
and immune to pain.

I'm twenty now,
cowering in an unknown time
waiting for my princess dresses to fit again,
waiting for the next rainfall,
watching the streetlights turn on,
and missing the smell of fresh-cut grass
drenched in laughter.

ASLEEP IN OCTOBER

I think you and I
are better off as
old friends.

As beautiful as it was
to be close to you
the sparks that lit between us,
they blazed us bare.
Burns scattered like fingerprints
or else constellations
only now engraved.

You're too like me
to be too close
though I just can't say no
            not to you, dear.

So old friends is all we can be
I will never deafen to your call
crawling back
in fear of becoming
strangers.

HOMESICK

I'm in my bed, under the roof that has watched me grow
surrounded by walls
that hold pictures of my friends
and postcards from people I used to know,
but I don't feel familiar.

the moon visits to catch my tears
as she does when I need her most,
and she asks me
with a disheartened grit in her voice
What brings you such sorrow?
to her gaze and say
I want to go home.
though I know this is my house-
the place that I have grown,
but something isn't quite right.

I do not know where to go
when I wish to go home.

Is it love

When coated with desperation?

If you asked them to love you again, would they?

Is it love if you have to ask?

UNTITLED #0210

Before me,
only the sun kissed the bridge of your nose
with enough light to shine
through a whole galaxy,
perfectly illuminating
every edge and curve
that you find distasteful,
but I find charming,

In your eyes,
I saw the woods I grew up in
the detailed oak
with etchings from people
who stood here long before we had passed through.

In your eyes
I see the cabin you grew up in
with the dusted window sills
and wrinkled cotton sheets

I can still smell the linen on you.

The sun peeks through again
and kisses your nose.
She will always do for me
what I am unable to

I'll thank her before us
and after we say goodbye.

SONGBIRD

If I could write to you
every word with an endearing undertone
I would
I'd string them up
like fairy lights
so in the night, when it's cold
you can feel my warmth
surrounding all of you

My love,
My light,

it's a product of your design

My love,
My light,

my heart is yours in all due time.

I AM ALREADY ALIVE

In bursts of laughter, I am smiling and
Almost becoming the second before quiet breaks and
Makes tears fall gleefully, and our ribs bruise.
Anything can bring me the decadence of life or
Light. I treasure it more than I have
Recently. After everything nearly
Ended, we learned to suck the nectar
Adoringly to appreciate the
Depth of life.
Yesterday will never be ours again-
Decidedly frivolous with our time.
Eventually, today will be yesterday, and we
Cannot change a thing about it. We will never be this
Alive again, and my god, are
You and I alive.
I will
Never be this young again, and I will learn to
Gulp the life out of the emptiest of cups.

LEGACY OF THE SOUL

I do not wish to have my body
a temple.
there is no worship
no stained glass,
or verses.
I will not be ignorant
to the pain outside,
I know I cannot wish it afar.
I will not let hate be born in my walls
then spread,
and prayed away.

I think I will be a home.
I find that much more appealing.

THE TROUBLED POET / THE DAMNED ARTIST

Both share a cigarette on the back porch
disturbingly inquisitive of what creates pain
and what pain creates.

The poet's mouth spews imagery of an injured bird
cradled in calloused hands.
How struggle can only be treated by those who have
suffered.

the artist's hands drip with graphite onto a fresh page
both experiencing the same exact thing-
collateral damage
created between the spoken and unsaid.
the poet lets go of nothing,
every feeling frozen in time
lingering for eternity
and the artist would rather be damned than let the poet
journey into the idea alone.

The ashes burn their knuckles,
and the lighter sparks again.

AN ACT OF GENTLENESS

One of our first conversations
was about pomegranates.
You had found a sale and seized the given opportunity.
nearly proud of yourself,
you said you hadn't a clue on how to eat it-
clueless to the art of breaking husk
and sparing the delicacy inside.

I had learned the art years before
from a woman with kind hands
my heart holding to the practice,
waiting for this exact moment.

Gently, I said.
maybe it's worth the taken time,
it is sweeter after the wait.
Let me prepare you a pomegranate.
Let's be gentle.

YOU ARE ALREADY WHOLE

It must be known to you that
there is no obligation for consumption

You are already whole.

There is no need for you to bleed yourself dry
or cut your hair to only wish it comes back
ten-fold after a performance of grand sacrifice
and how well you cleaned up afterward

You are already whole.

Your hips do not indent solely
for ensnaring or childbearing,
they work in tandem with every part of *you*
to run and dance or simply to express

You are already whole.

Another heart does not make yours
more than it was before
Every part of your core
has always been here
without exception, your giggle
and blush of love has been
engrained into you
at the first beat of your heart

You are whole.
You always have been.

A LIFE LIVED

Before I'm gone, tell them
I was a kid with so many words
and so little space to put them.

tell them I was a mirrorball of
things heard and seen

therefore absorbed into some
unreadable constellation

with the curiosity of a feline
on its seventh life-

the first six wasted wisely
the last three surely to go the same.

Tell them how a smile laid
smitten at the bottom of every wine glass I owned.

I was never a quiet lover
but white grapes apiece
met my mouth as a microphone
amplifying giggles, glimmers and every

god, I could look at you forever

Tell them I was vineyard sweet.

before I am gone, tell them that
I was a secret door hidden with a trophy showcase.

for who would test such
delicate things

when they whisper the sweetest nothings
bouncing off plexiglass-

A protective feature, really.

After I am gone,
give them this map to get in,
let them find their own way out.

ALL ALONG, WE WERE BLOOMING

When we first met
I pulled fun at the thought of an invisible string
yanking the threads separate
to sew my skepticism secure.
The foolish me
dancing around
my vacant seamstress skills,
            I picked up gardening instead.

I packed all the things that challenged me
deep beneath the muddy pessimism
out of sight, out of mind, right
burying them deeper and deeper with my two left feet
and my blissfully ignorant attitude
        a buffoon with strings now deep underground.

Do you think I struggled before you
to know you better?
Living a booze-induced seventeen
finding fragments
        of the old you in the old me.

To think of all I learned the hard way
so holding you would come easy
it's hard not to think
that as I stood strong above,
all along, we were blooming.

ARALIACEAE

What a pleasure it has been
to know you
I am painfully aware of how things change
And how vile time can be with how short life is.

I am grateful I will always have a corner of my heart
Decorated with the stories you've painted
Sure, you'll create so many more
That I will never see
and I'm certain in time, you will invent a new colour, but
the ones I hold will never fade.

You'll change perfumes
When the smell starts to turn your stomach
Or the last drop is used sparingly,
But each time I pass someone
Coated in the sweet daffodil aroma,
I'll hear you sing.
How blissful it has been
To grow apart from you.

LIGHT BULB

If ghosts are real, I hope my lights flicker
and each time they wink off,
they blink on twice as bright.
I hope I can find the contemporary dance
between here and never-
tripping the light fantastic
in the pleasant absence of before.

I wonder if I go first
how could I manufacture my presence ·
into something warm?
Ghosts are known for a chill down your spine,
lurking in the dark,
hiding blind,
but do you think, if I really tried
I could appear as a flick
in your candle wick
as you sit down to write
almost saying

ooh, I like that line
keep writing, keep trying, keeping me alive.

Do you think someone has to die in order
to carry a piece of them
in shimmers you find?

because I'm certain I am already a ghost
in some old friends' eyes-
truly, that's fine
I pass through their thoughts as they do in mine
a lasting 'blast from the past'
perhaps a haunting?
anyhow,
I digress.
I would like to believe ghosts are real,
it makes changing the bulbs
a bit more enticing.

PIGEON

Another version of me lives in Montreal
born there, and left behind
in an airport chair
with an incorrectly guided ticket.
She didn't care
as there was no rush in Montreal,
at least not for her.
And that is partially the reason
I had to leave her behind.

I am terrified of change,
she is petrified
I will stay this way forever
It's exhilarating to have no idea
Where you are,
or where you might end up going.

I've lived this way for years
and have only recently found familiarity at home.
I know which cars
I will pass on my way to work
and how to never hit a red on the way back.

I know this town
like the back of my shaking hand
that operates the only version
of myself I recognize.
I know which bleak shirt I will pair
with a spiffy pair of pants.
I know I will stay tethered to anything that
tugs me hard enough

I know everything I own is shaded
with the neutrality of my landlocked town.

But in Montreal,
I wore red.

PROMETHEUS' PROCLAMATION

Yesterday, I realized you had a body
And if tomorrow I've forgotten,
allow me to embrace the return
Of what I do not need to be shown
For if my hands were forbid from caressing the slope of
your sun-stained nose
my love would not waiver, as I know
I don't need to feel you want to stay
you've been threaded into all of my senses
and seams

I do not need to touch you to love you
You are a burning ball of light, and I,
Prometheus would string up the hands
that preserve the life of man
Just to hear the crackle of embers and ardour from
across the sky
However selfish, I love you for all that you are
Not what you can give to me

My love is pure.
You are plenty.

MEMENTO VIVERE

Listen closely now, as tomorrow branches over the hill
I've watched the sun dip low, the weight of every
yesterday compiling.
In my hands, the echoes of moments long prior,
A tapestry woven with mirth and thick sighs.

You shutter at time passing, of the shadows it casts,
Though within each sunset, beauty tranquilly lingers.
Remember the bliss of a first kiss
The early taste of love, a sweet,
fleeting delight.

Embrace each goodbye, even when it stings
For those tender moments shape who you'll become.
Every farewell is part of life's dance
A reminder to cherish every beat in your chest,
every chance.

It is fragile, as dandelion tufts caught in the fall breeze,
And it's in that impermanence that we breathe in life.
Do not shy away from shadows; let them teach you grace,
For each moment is a whisper, a treasure to hold dear.

When you feel time rushing, remember the greatest gift we
have all been given and fill your lungs with it.
Let the eventide revive you to the ripeness of fading light.
The moments you treasure, though they may not last,
It is the *nevermore* that softens what's remembered.

So, as you step forward now, courage in hand,
Know that time is not a thief,
But a gentle teacher.
Live fully, and love deeply as each moment unfolds
Delicate and unforgiving
For the essence of life is each thread that we weave,
its beauty laid bare.
We can never return to this last-passing second
Savour it later, as for now, we are living.

THREE COUNT RHYTHM

I am a lover
my heart larger than my head.
I am an artist
no light goes unnoticed.

I am here.
I am alive.

I hope to be here long after I am gone.
My heart will still beat.

Hold it in your hands now-
flip the page.

I am here.
I am alive.

CURTAIN CALL

I hope when I come to the end of my life

I'll be able to laugh along

with the rhythm of my heart monitor.

I hope I can say

"I had so much fun, and I'm glad I can rest"

ACKNOWLEDGEMENTS

Coming to the end of this, I must express my deepest gratitude towards a couple of extraordinary people. To my family- my mom, dad, papa, and grandma for their absolute patience with me and my wild dreams of becoming an author. I hope to make you proud.

To Atlas, my best friend, who believed in me way before they had any reason to. Thank you for the endless support, the laughter and the memories. You have always been a light to me. I don't believe I would be the person I am now without you beside me. Thank you for making me taste life in ways I had never considered. I hope you get back tenfold all the love and acceptance you put out in the world. I love you.

To Zeb, your creative spirit has influenced much of my own work, and I think that is one of the greatest gifts you can give an artist. Thank you for listening to me ramble out ideas and congratulating my small victories when I'm too stuck in the big picture. I love you.

To the ones I loved and lost. Thank you for inspiring my work and teaching me that love is never gone- grief is only an extension of what was. To all who contributed to the making of this book— in ways big or small, seen or unseen— this work is as much yours as it is mine.

I dedicate this book to you all. I love you, thank you for being alive.

ABOUT THE AUTHOR

Eva Froess is an independent Canadian author and poet. She began her focus on poetry in 2018, though when she's not writing, Eva can be found exploring around British Columbia and spending quality time with her loved ones. Her passion is healing through creativity, and she hopes even one of her readers is impacted by her work.

www.ingramcontent.com/pod-product-compliance
Lightning Source LLC
LaVergne TN
LVHW041058150826
845673LV00007B/1834

* 9 7 8 1 0 6 9 1 0 5 9 0 5 *